AI Powered Marketing

How Artificial Intelligence Will Revolutionize Marketing, Advertising and media.

Copyright © Hebooks rights reserved,
this book or any portion thereof may not be
reproduced or used in any manner whatsoever without
permission of the publisher

Chapters

Chapter 1 : Introduction

Chapter 2 : Fundamentals of AI

Chapter 3 : Personalized Marketing

Chapter 4 : Predictive Analytics

Chapter 5 : Chatbots

Chapter 6 : AI in Content Creatio

Chapter 7 : Ethical Considerations

Chapter 8 : The Road Ahead

Chapter 9 : Implementing AI in Marketing

Chapter 1 : Introduction

In the fast-evolving landscape of contemporary marketing, Artificial Intelligence (AI) takes center stage as a sophisticated technology, amalgamating various components that imitate human cognitive processes within the domain of machines. At its core lie foundational elements such as machine learning, natural language processing (NLP), and predictive analytics. Machine learning endows AI systems with the ability to discern patterns and make predictions based on extensive data analysis. On the other hand, NLP facilitates AI in comprehending, interpreting, and generating human language, thereby fostering seamless communication between machines and individuals. Predictive analytics leverages AI's computational prowess to forecast future trends and behaviors by scrutinizing historical data.

The relevance of AI in today's dynamic business landscape is paramount. With the explosive proliferation of digital data and the widespread adoption of online platforms, businesses grapple with an enormous challenge of interpreting and deriving meaningful insights from the sheer volume of available information. In this scenario, AI emerges as a solution, adeptly processing and analyzing data to extract valuable insights. These insights, in turn, enable businesses to make informed marketing decisions by providing a comprehensive understanding of consumer behaviors, preferences, and prevailing market trends. AI's ability to distill meaningful insights significantly amplifies customer engagement by allowing the tailoring of marketing strategies to specific audience segments, thus establishing a profound and personalized connection with customers. Consequently, AI has swiftly transitioned from a novel concept to an indispensable tool, propelling marketing strategies into an era characterized by unparalleled precision and effectiveness.

AI's integration into marketing practices has evolved significantly since its inception in the mid-20th century. The journey began with foundational research in the 1950s, where AI emerged as an academic field. Early attempts at utilizing AI in marketing were modest due to the limitations in computational capabilities and the scarcity of data. However, pioneers recognized the potential of AI in transforming marketing strategies and embarked on a journey to explore its applications.

During the 1980s and 1990s, advancements in computing technology paved the way for more comprehensive applications of AI in marketing. Researchers and marketers started to experiment with AI techniques to automate certain marketing tasks and optimize decision-making processes. These efforts laid the groundwork for the integration of AI into customer relationship management (CRM) systems, enabling businesses to better understand and serve their customers.

The 21st century witnessed a rapid acceleration in AI's integration into marketing strategies. Breakthroughs in machine learning and deep learning significantly bolstered AI's ability to analyze vast amounts of data. Notable milestones include the development of sophisticated algorithms that enhanced customer segmentation, predictive analytics, and personalization, thus enabling businesses to tailor their marketing efforts to specific target audiences.

Key individuals and organizations played pivotal roles in pioneering the application of AI in marketing. Visionaries like John McCarthy, Marvin Minsky, and Philip Kotler advocated for AI's potential in transforming marketing practices. Organizations started investing heavily in AI research and development, paving the way for cutting-edge marketing solutions. This historical journey sets the stage for understanding how AI has evolved from its infancy to become an integral part of contemporary marketing strategies.

In the present landscape of marketing, Artificial Intelligence (AI) stands as a pivotal tool, wielding a profound influence on how businesses engage with consumers and devise strategies to promote their products or services. Its significance lies in its ability to process and analyze colossal volumes of data swiftly and accurately. Through AI-driven analytics, businesses gain invaluable insights into consumer behaviors, preferences, and trends, empowering them to make data-driven decisions and formulate highly targeted and personalized marketing strategies.

One of the primary impacts of AI in modern marketing is the automation of various processes, saving both time and resources. AI-powered marketing tools and platforms can automate tasks such as email campaigns, social media posting, and customer segmentation, enabling marketing teams to focus on more strategic and creative aspects. Moreover, AI algorithms can intelligently optimize advertising campaigns, ensuring that marketing efforts are efficiently directed towards the right audience at the right time.

Personalization, a cornerstone of effective marketing, is significantly enhanced by AI. By leveraging AI's analytical capabilities, businesses can tailor their marketing content to specific customer segments, thereby increasing engagement and conversion rates. AI-powered chatbots and virtual assistants offer personalized customer interactions, enhancing overall customer experience and fostering brand loyalty.

Ultimately, the integration of AI into marketing strategies leads to enhanced return on investment (ROI). By optimizing marketing campaigns, identifying high-converting channels, and providing deep insights into consumer behavior, AI helps businesses allocate their marketing resources effectively. This ensures that marketing efforts generate the maximum impact and drive business growth. The profound significance of AI in modern marketing cannot be understated, as it stands at the forefront of a technological revolution that is reshaping the marketing landscape.

The infusion of Artificial Intelligence (AI) into marketing strategies has heralded a transformative era, fundamentally altering how businesses interact with their audience and navigate the competitive market. At the heart of this transformation lies AI's capacity to automate routine and laborious tasks, freeing up valuable time and resources for marketers to focus on strategy and creativity. AI-powered tools and algorithms handle data analysis, trend monitoring, and campaign optimization seamlessly, contributing to more efficient and effective marketing operations.

One of AI's hallmark contributions to marketing is the personalization of customer experiences. By employing sophisticated algorithms, businesses can precisely tailor their messages, advertisements, and offerings to match the unique preferences and behaviors of individual consumers. From targeted ads based on browsing history to personalized product recommendations, AI ensures that every interaction resonates with customers, thereby enhancing engagement and fostering brand loyalty.

Moreover, AI's predictive capabilities are reshaping how businesses anticipate consumer behavior. Through analyzing historical data and real-time interactions, AI algorithms forecast trends and consumer responses. This foresight equips marketers with invaluable insights to align their strategies, content, and products with emerging market demands, gaining a competitive edge.

The transformative power of AI extends across various facets of marketing. In advertising, AI facilitates programmatic advertising, where real-time bidding and ad placements are optimized based on user behavior and preferences. AI-driven content creation tools assist in generating compelling narratives, videos, and visuals, streamlining content development and amplifying engagement. Additionally, AI-powered chatbots and virtual assistants revolutionize customer service by providing instant and personalized support around the clock, enhancing overall customer satisfaction.

As a result of these advancements, the marketing landscape is evolving into a dynamic and data-driven ecosystem, where businesses can establish deeper connections with their audience and innovate their strategies based on actionable insights. AI is driving a paradigm shift, redefining marketing norms and propelling businesses towards a future where customer-centricity and efficiency reign supreme.

Chapter 2 : Fundamentals of AI

Machine Learning (ML) stands as a cornerstone in the realm of Artificial Intelligence (AI), providing systems the ability to learn and improve their performance without being explicitly programmed. At its core, machine learning involves the development of algorithms and models that enable computers to identify patterns and glean insights from vast amounts of data. This ability to learn and adapt is what sets machine learning apart and empowers AI to simulate human-like decision-making.

Machine learning algorithms function by analyzing historical data to identify patterns and make predictions or decisions based on new input. They improve their performance over time through an iterative process of learning from data, making adjustments, and optimizing their models. This process is often referred to as "training" the machine learning model.

The types of machine learning approaches can be broadly categorized into three main types:

Supervised Learning: In supervised learning, the algorithm is trained using labeled data, meaning each input is associated with a corresponding desired output. The algorithm learns to map the inputs to the correct outputs and can then make predictions on new, unseen data.

Unsupervised Learning: Unsupervised learning involves using unlabeled data where the algorithm identifies patterns and structures on its own. It groups similar data points together, enabling insights into the inherent structure of the data.

Reinforcement Learning: Reinforcement learning operates on the principle of an agent interacting with an environment. The agent learns to take specific actions to maximize a reward signal obtained from the environment, essentially learning optimal strategies through trial and error.

Understanding these concepts is pivotal for comprehending AI's capabilities and its potential for revolutionizing various domains, including marketing strategies, by leveraging the power of machine learning algorithms.

Neural networks, inspired by the human brain's structure and functioning, are fundamental building blocks of modern artificial intelligence. At its essence, a neural network is composed of interconnected nodes, called neurons, arranged in layers. The connections between these neurons are numerical weights that determine the strength and impact of signals as they pass through the network.

The structure of a neural network consists of three main types of layers:

Input Layer: This layer receives the initial data or features that are fed into the network. Each neuron in the input layer represents a specific feature of the input data.

Hidden Layers: Between the input and output layers, there can be one or more hidden layers. Hidden layers allow the network to learn complex representations and patterns from the input data.

Output Layer: The final layer of the network produces the output based on the learned patterns and representations. The number of neurons in the output layer is determined by the type of problem being addressed (e.g., binary classification, multi-class classification).

The activation function in a neural network introduces non-linearity into the model, enabling the network to learn complex relationships and patterns within the data. Activation functions are applied to the weighted sum of inputs for each neuron in a layer, determining the neuron's output. Common activation functions include the sigmoid function, ReLU (Rectified Linear Unit), and tanh (hyperbolic tangent).

Training a neural network involves adjusting the weights of connections to minimize the difference between predicted outputs and actual outputs. This process is achieved through backpropagation, where the error in the predictions is propagated back through the network, and gradient descent algorithms are utilized to adjust the weights iteratively. Gradient descent calculates the gradient of the error with respect to each weight, indicating the direction and magnitude of the weight adjustments required to minimize the error.

Understanding the structure and operations of neural networks is foundational to comprehending how AI systems process and learn from data, making them a critical tool in the advancement of AI applications across various domains.

Deep learning stands at the pinnacle of AI, representing a subfield dedicated to handling intricate, large-scale data. It has gained immense significance due to its ability to discern patterns and features from diverse data types, which include images, text, and sound. The term "deep" refers to the numerous layers within a deep neural network (DNN), distinguishing it from traditional machine learning models. These multiple layers allow deep neural networks to abstract high-level representations of data in a hierarchical fashion.

The architecture of deep neural networks mirrors the complexity of the human brain. Each layer of neurons is akin to a level of abstraction, extracting progressively intricate features from the input data. In this hierarchical arrangement, the initial layers detect elementary features, such as edges in an image, while subsequent layers amalgamate these features to recognize more complex structures like shapes and eventually whole objects. This hierarchical extraction of features through the layers is fundamental to the success and effectiveness of deep learning models.

The significance of deep learning lies in its unparalleled performance in various AI applications. Deep neural networks have excelled in tasks like image and speech recognition, natural language processing, recommendation systems, and autonomous vehicles. The deep learning approach differs from traditional machine learning as it automates the feature engineering process. Rather than relying on handcrafted features, deep learning models autonomously learn and extract features from raw data, presenting a revolutionary shift in the field of AI.

For instance, in image recognition, instead of crafting features like edges and textures manually, a deep learning model learns these features through its layers, allowing it to discern intricate patterns and objects with remarkable accuracy. This autonomy in feature extraction has propelled deep learning to the forefront of AI research and applications.

Understanding the principles and potential of deep learning is essential for grasping how AI systems can process extensive data, revealing underlying patterns that were previously elusive. As we delve further into the book, we will explore how this understanding forms the basis for applying deep learning techniques to revolutionize marketing strategies and consumer engagement.

Supervised and unsupervised learning are foundational paradigms in machine learning, distinguished primarily by their approaches to data processing and learning.

In supervised learning, the model is trained using labeled data, wherein each data point is accompanied by the correct output. The algorithm learns to map the input data to the corresponding desired output through an iterative optimization process. Essentially, the model is guided by a teacher (the labeled data) during training, allowing it to make predictions or classify new, unseen data accurately.

Contrastingly, unsupervised learning operates without labeled data. The model explores the inherent patterns and structures within the data on its own. The algorithm identifies similarities and differences, clustering similar data points together to uncover underlying patterns without any predefined guidance. Unsupervised learning is particularly beneficial when the objective is to explore the data's intrinsic properties and extract meaningful insights without any prior knowledge of expected outcomes.

In the context of marketing, supervised learning can be employed for sentiment analysis of customer reviews. By training the model on labeled data where sentiments are categorized (e.g., positive, negative, neutral), the algorithm learns to predict sentiment for new, unclassified reviews, providing businesses with valuable insights into consumer perceptions.

On the other hand, unsupervised learning finds application in customer segmentation. Using clustering techniques, it groups customers based on their behaviors, preferences, or purchase histories. This segmentation enables businesses to tailor marketing strategies for different customer segments, optimizing engagement and conversions.

Understanding the distinctions between supervised and unsupervised learning is critical, as their appropriate application can significantly impact the effectiveness of AI solutions in various domains, including marketing. The ability to choose the right learning paradigm based on the problem at hand is a fundamental skill for any AI practitioner.

Artificial Intelligence (AI) fundamentals, including machine learning, neural networks, and deep learning, have emerged as transformative tools in the marketing domain, enhancing strategies and elevating customer engagement to new heights.

Machine learning, a fundamental component, plays a pivotal role in customer segmentation. By analyzing vast amounts of data, machine learning algorithms identify distinct customer segments based on various parameters such as behavior, demographics, and preferences. This segmentation allows businesses to tailor their marketing efforts to specific target audiences, optimizing the relevance and effectiveness of marketing campaigns.

Neural networks, inspired by the human brain's structure, excel in recommendation systems. These systems process vast amounts of data to understand customer preferences and behaviors. By leveraging intricate patterns and user interactions, neural networks provide tailored recommendations, significantly impacting purchase decisions. For instance, e-commerce platforms use recommendation systems to suggest products based on a user's browsing and purchasing history.

Deep learning, with its ability to handle complex data and hierarchically extract features, has revolutionized sentiment analysis. By processing text data from reviews, social media, or customer feedback, deep learning models can discern sentiment polarity, identifying positive, negative, or neutral sentiments. This analysis aids businesses in gauging consumer perceptions, enabling them to adapt marketing strategies accordingly.

The dichotomy of supervised and unsupervised learning is instrumental in optimizing marketing strategies. Supervised learning guides customer engagement strategies by predicting customer responses to various campaigns, allowing businesses to tailor their approach. Conversely, unsupervised learning, especially clustering, helps identify segments with similar behaviors or preferences, aiding in targeted marketing and personalization.

The integration of AI fundamentals in marketing is transformative. These technologies empower businesses to analyze vast amounts of data, extract valuable insights, and tailor strategies to engage customers effectively. As we delve deeper into this book, we will explore specific applications and use cases where AI in marketing has made a substantial impact, propelling the industry towards unparalleled growth and innovation.

As the landscape of AI continually evolves, recent advancements in machine learning and deep learning have been at the forefront, shaping the future of artificial intelligence and its applications across various domains, including marketing.

Transfer learning has emerged as a powerful paradigm in machine learning. It involves pre-training a model on a large dataset and then fine-tuning it for a specific task. This approach leverages the knowledge gained from the pre-training stage, significantly reducing the data and resources required to achieve high performance in subsequent tasks. Transfer learning is particularly valuable in scenarios where labeled data is limited, allowing for efficient model training and deployment.

Generative Adversarial Networks (GANs) represent a groundbreaking concept in deep learning. GANs consist of two neural networks, the generator and the discriminator, trained simultaneously through adversarial training. The generator creates data resembling the real dataset, aiming to deceive the discriminator, which, in turn, distinguishes between real and generated data. GANs have found applications in generating realistic images, enhancing image resolution, creating artwork, and even in data augmentation, contributing to advancements in several domains.

These emerging trends are set to redefine the landscape of AI, with potential implications for marketing strategies. Transfer learning allows for more efficient and effective model training for marketing-specific tasks, such as customer segmentation or sentiment analysis. By leveraging pre-trained models, businesses can derive insights and optimize their strategies with smaller, domain-specific datasets.

GANs offer exciting prospects for content creation and personalization in marketing. They can be utilized to generate realistic visuals, enhance advertising creativity, and personalize user experiences. For instance, GANs can aid in creating personalized advertisements tailored to individual preferences, ultimately enhancing engagement and conversion rates.

Staying abreast of these emerging trends in AI fundamentals is vital for both AI practitioners and marketers. These advancements hold significant promise, shaping the trajectory of AI and its potential impact on marketing strategies. As we progress through this book, we will delve deeper into these trends, exploring their applications and potential in reshaping the marketing landscape.

Chapter 3 : Personalized Marketing

Personalized marketing leverages sophisticated algorithms to deliver tailored experiences and recommendations to individual consumers. These algorithms can be broadly categorized into three main types: collaborative filtering, content-based filtering, and hybrid approaches.

Collaborative Filtering:

Collaborative filtering relies on user-item interactions to make recommendations. It identifies patterns and preferences based on the actions and behaviors of similar users. The fundamental idea is that if two users have similar preferences for certain items, they are likely to have similar preferences for other items as well. Collaborative filtering can be user-based or item-based. User-based filtering recommends items to a user based on what similar users have liked, while item-based filtering recommends items similar to those a user has shown interest in.

Content-Based Filtering:

Content-based filtering recommends items based on the characteristics or attributes of the items themselves. It focuses on analyzing the content, features, or properties of items and aligning them with a user's historical preferences. This approach is particularly effective in suggesting items that are similar in content or characteristics to those a user has previously interacted with. It's especially useful when there is a lot of data available about the items.

Hybrid Approaches:

Hybrid approaches combine elements of both collaborative filtering and content-based filtering to provide more accurate and diversified recommendations. By leveraging the strengths of both approaches, hybrid systems attempt to mitigate the limitations of individual algorithms. Hybrid models are versatile and can adapt to various scenarios, ensuring better recommendations by considering both user interactions and item attributes.

These algorithms analyze vast amounts of customer data and behaviors to understand preferences, interactions, and patterns. Collaborative filtering identifies users with similar tastes, recommending items based on what others with similar preferences have liked. Content-based filtering, on the other hand, assesses the features of the items and recommends based on similarity in characteristics. Hybrid approaches blend these strategies, utilizing the power of both collaborative and content-based filtering.

The strengths of collaborative filtering lie in its ability to provide serendipitous recommendations and handle new items or users effectively. Content-based filtering excels in recommending niche or less popular items. Hybrid approaches strike a balance, offering a wider range of recommendations, enhancing overall user satisfaction.

In different personalized marketing scenarios, the choice of algorithm depends on the nature of the data, the context of recommendation, and the desired level of personalization. Collaborative filtering often works well in scenarios with substantial user interaction data, while content-based filtering shines when detailed item information is available. Hybrid approaches offer a flexible solution, adaptable to various contexts, and are often preferred in diverse and evolving marketing landscapes.

Understanding these algorithms is crucial for effectively tailoring marketing messages and recommendations, ultimately enhancing customer engagement and driving business success.

Personalized marketing serves as a transformative strategy that profoundly influences consumer engagement and purchasing behavior. At its core, the impact of personalization lies in the tailored experiences and recommendations provided to individual consumers based on their preferences, behaviors, and demographics. Consumers are drawn to personalized content because it resonates with them, grabbing their attention and fostering a sense of exclusivity and value. When consumers perceive that a brand understands their needs and preferences, they are more likely to engage with the content, spending more time on websites or platforms and exhibiting higher interaction rates.

Moreover, personalized marketing significantly impacts purchasing behavior. Consumers are more inclined to make a purchase when presented with products or services that align with their preferences and past behaviors. Recommendations based on their purchase history or similar consumer patterns instill confidence and reduce decision fatigue. Personalized offers, discounts, or incentives create a sense of urgency and encourage immediate action, ultimately driving conversions and boosting sales.

Psychological aspects play a pivotal role in the effectiveness of personalized content. The mere perception of being understood and valued triggers a positive emotional response, contributing to a stronger affinity for the brand or product. The psychological phenomenon known as the "mere exposure effect" further reinforces this, as consumers tend to develop a preference for things they are exposed to more frequently. Personalized content aligns with this principle, exposing individuals to content that resonates with their preferences and thereby enhancing their affinity and inclination towards the brand or product.

Supported by numerous case studies and research findings, the positive impact of personalized marketing is evident. For instance, a study by Accenture revealed that 91% of consumers are more likely to shop with brands that provide relevant offers and recommendations. Industry giants like Amazon, Spotify, and Netflix have successfully leveraged personalization, significantly increasing user engagement and retention rates. These empirical insights, combined with the psychological underpinnings, underscore the significance of personalization in creating a more impactful and fruitful relationship between businesses and consumers.

Real-world examples vividly demonstrate the potent impact of AI-driven personalized marketing in diverse industries. Industry leaders have effectively harnessed AI algorithms and customer data to provide tailored experiences, products, or services, showcasing the transformative potential of personalization.

One notable example is Amazon, a pioneer in personalized marketing. Amazon's recommendation engine, powered by AI algorithms, analyzes a user's browsing and purchase history to suggest products that align with their preferences. This approach significantly enhances user engagement and drives sales, accounting for a substantial portion of

Amazon's revenue. The success of their recommendation system is a testament to the power of personalization and AI in shaping consumer behavior.

Another exemplar is Netflix, a streaming service that utilizes AI algorithms to curate personalized recommendations for each user. By analyzing a user's viewing history and behavior, Netflix suggests movies and shows tailored to individual tastes, keeping users engaged and encouraging continued subscriptions. This personalized recommendation engine has been instrumental in retaining a massive user base and fueling the success of the platform.

Spotify, a leading music streaming service, also employs AI for personalization. Their algorithms analyze a user's listening history to create personalized playlists and recommend new songs and artists. This highly personalized experience not only keeps users engaged but also encourages them to explore and discover new music, contributing to increased user satisfaction and loyalty.

The outcomes of these personalized marketing initiatives are remarkable. These companies have witnessed substantial improvements in customer engagement, satisfaction, and ultimately, their bottom line. The return on investment (ROI) has been substantial, with increased user interactions, longer session times, and higher conversion rates. Customer satisfaction metrics, such as Net Promoter Score (NPS), have also shown significant improvements, indicating the positive impact of personalized marketing on overall customer experience.

These real-world examples demonstrate the immense potential of AI-driven personalized marketing. By leveraging customer data and AI algorithms, companies can deliver tailored experiences that resonate with individual preferences, ultimately driving business success and fostering lasting customer relationships.

Personalized marketing, a potent tool in engaging consumers effectively, brings forth a set of ethical considerations. Chief among these is the delicate balance between personalization and consumer privacy. In the relentless quest to tailor experiences, products, and services to individual preferences, businesses often grapple with the challenge of safeguarding consumer data privacy and ensuring robust data security measures.

One of the most pressing ethical concerns pertains to privacy and data security. The accumulation of extensive consumer data, fundamental for personalization, raises questions about how this data is gathered, stored, and utilized. Consumers rightfully worry about the security measures in place to protect their data from potential breaches and unauthorized access. Maintaining the trust of consumers involves addressing these concerns and prioritizing data security to prevent identity theft, fraud, or any form of privacy infringement.

Striking the right balance between personalization and privacy is crucial for ethical personalized marketing. Consumers appreciate personalized recommendations and offerings as long as they feel in control of their data. This necessitates transparency in data collection practices and providing consumers with the option to consent or opt out of personalized marketing. Respecting the privacy choices of individuals ensures that personalization is conducted ethically and with their interests and consent at the forefront, fostering a relationship of trust between businesses and consumers.

To uphold ethical standards, businesses should adhere to a set of best practices and guidelines. Transparency emerges as a key principle, necessitating clear and accessible privacy policies that elucidate how consumer data is utilized. Obtaining explicit consent from consumers before leveraging their data for personalization is foundational. Robust data security measures are imperative, ensuring that consumer data is handled and stored securely, mitigating potential risks and demonstrating commitment to consumer privacy.

Additionally, embracing the principle of data minimization is essential. This entails collecting only the data that is necessary for personalization, avoiding unnecessary or excessive data gathering. Regular audits and compliance checks, coupled with staying informed about evolving privacy laws and regulations, are critical in upholding ethical practices within the realm of personalized marketing.

Ethical considerations are paramount in personalized marketing. Balancing personalization with privacy, ensuring data security, and adhering to ethical guidelines are foundational for businesses seeking to deliver personalized experiences while upholding ethical standards and building enduring trust with consumers.

The future of personalized marketing is teeming with exciting prospects, driven by emerging trends and cutting-edge technologies. As AI continues to evolve, its symbiotic relationship with marketing is expected to reach new heights, revolutionizing how businesses engage with consumers.

Emerging Trends and Technologies:

Emerging trends are set to shape the trajectory of personalized marketing. Augmented Reality (AR) and Virtual Reality (VR) are gaining prominence, offering immersive, personalized experiences to consumers. These technologies allow customers to virtually experience products before making a purchase, enhancing their engagement and confidence in their buying decisions. Additionally, Internet of Things (IoT) devices are creating a vast ecosystem of interconnected devices, enabling personalized marketing opportunities based on real-time data from these devices.

Advancements in AI, Machine Learning, and Data Analytics:

Advancements in AI, machine learning, and data analytics will be the cornerstone of future personalized marketing. AI algorithms will become increasingly sophisticated, enabling deeper insights into consumer behavior and preferences. Machine learning models will be capable of real-time learning and adaptation, ensuring that recommendations and personalization remain up-to-date and relevant. Advanced data analytics will provide a comprehensive understanding of consumer journeys, allowing businesses to anticipate needs and tailor their strategies accordingly.

Hyper-Personalization and Its Impact:

Hyper-personalization is poised to redefine marketing strategies and consumer experiences. It involves creating highly individualized experiences for each consumer, going beyond traditional personalization. By leveraging AI to analyze vast amounts of data, businesses can anticipate specific consumer needs, preferences, and behaviors. This level of personalization enables precisely targeted marketing messages, product recommendations, and offers. Consequently, consumers feel a deeper connection with brands, driving increased engagement, customer loyalty, and ultimately, business growth.

The potential impact of hyper-personalization on marketing strategies is immense. Marketing campaigns will become incredibly precise, resonating with each individual consumer. Brands will be able to forge genuine relationships with consumers by demonstrating an acute understanding of their unique preferences. Moreover, hyper-personalization can lead to a significant reduction in marketing waste, optimizing resources and improving ROI.

The future of personalized marketing is marked by dynamic trends and advancements in technology. As we move forward, harnessing the power of AI, machine learning, and data analytics will be pivotal in achieving hyper-personalization. This paradigm shift is set to transform marketing strategies, delivering unparalleled consumer experiences and cementing a new era of marketing effectiveness and efficiency.

Chapter 4 : Predictive Analytics

Predictive analytics is a potent tool within the marketing landscape, leveraging data and statistical algorithms to forecast future outcomes based on historical data and current trends. It entails a systematic process of analyzing data to identify patterns, assess trends, and make informed predictions. In the realm of marketing, predictive analytics holds immense relevance, providing a forward-looking perspective that aids in strategic decision-making and campaign optimization.

Relevance in Marketing:

Predictive analytics revolutionizes marketing strategies by offering valuable insights into consumer behaviors and preferences. By examining past interactions and purchase histories, businesses can anticipate future actions and trends. This insight enables marketers to tailor campaigns, content, and product offerings to align with what consumers are likely to respond to positively. From personalized recommendations to targeted advertising, predictive analytics shapes marketing approaches to be more precise, efficient, and ultimately, successful.

Key Concepts:

At the core of predictive analytics lie essential concepts such as data modeling, pattern recognition, and trend analysis. Data modeling involves the creation of models based on historical data, which are then used to predict future outcomes. Pattern recognition entails identifying recurring patterns within the data, offering a basis for predictions. Trend analysis helps in understanding the direction in which consumer preferences are evolving, facilitating proactive marketing strategies that stay ahead of market shifts.

Illustrative Examples:

Consider an e-commerce platform analyzing past purchase data and online behavior. Predictive analytics can identify patterns where certain customers frequently purchase particular products during seasonal sales. Armed with this insight, the platform can proactively target these customers with personalized promotions during the next seasonal sale, thereby maximizing engagement and sales.

In another scenario, a media streaming service utilizes predictive analytics to foresee content preferences. By analyzing viewing history and content types consumed, the service can suggest new shows or movies aligning with a user's preferences, enhancing user satisfaction and retention.

In both cases, predictive analytics, through data modeling and pattern analysis, helps in foreseeing consumer behaviors, enabling businesses to tailor their marketing strategies effectively.

Predictive analytics in marketing is a powerful compass that guides businesses in understanding and predicting consumer actions. It empowers marketers to make data-driven decisions, optimize campaigns, and deliver what consumers desire, ultimately boosting engagement and driving business success.

Artificial Intelligence (AI) is an indispensable tool that significantly enhances predictive analytics, ushering in a new era of precision and efficiency within marketing strategies. AI leverages advanced algorithms and computational power to analyze vast amounts of data, extract meaningful patterns, and generate predictions that form the backbone of predictive analytics in marketing.

Enhancing Predictive Analytics:

AI augments predictive analytics by enabling more sophisticated and accurate predictions. Through machine learning, AI algorithms continuously learn and adapt, improving their predictive capabilities over time. The ability to process immense volumes of data swiftly allows AI to identify intricate patterns that might go unnoticed through traditional analytics. AI's capacity to handle diverse data types, including structured and unstructured data, further enriches predictive models.

Common AI Techniques and Algorithms:

AI employs a range of techniques and algorithms in predictive analytics. Machine learning algorithms like decision trees, random forests, support vector machines, and neural networks are commonly used. Deep learning, a subset of machine learning, is gaining prominence for its prowess in handling complex, unstructured data. Natural Language Processing (NLP) is instrumental in sentiment analysis and understanding textual data. Additionally, reinforcement learning is evolving, enabling AI to make decisions by learning from interactions with its environment.

Advantages of Incorporating AI:

Incorporating AI into predictive analytics offers numerous advantages. AI-driven predictive models are often more accurate due to their ability to consider a multitude of variables and subtle patterns. These models adapt in real-time, reflecting changes in consumer behavior swiftly. Moreover, AI-powered predictive analytics provide a deeper understanding of consumer preferences and behaviors, facilitating precise targeting and personalization. This accuracy and precision ultimately lead to enhanced marketing decision-making, optimizing resource allocation and improving return on investment (ROI).

By embracing AI in predictive analytics, marketing strategies become data-driven and dynamic, propelling businesses towards a future where decisions are precise, timely, and perfectly aligned with consumer expectations.

Predictive analytics is a versatile tool with applications that significantly influence marketing strategies, aiding businesses in understanding, engaging, and retaining their target audience.

Customer Segmentation:

Predictive analytics plays a crucial role in customer segmentation, allowing businesses to categorize their customer base into distinct groups based on behavior, demographics, purchasing patterns, and other parameters. By understanding the unique preferences and characteristics of each segment, marketers can tailor their strategies, messaging, and offers to effectively target and engage these groups. This results in more personalized and impactful marketing campaigns, ultimately leading to higher conversion rates and customer satisfaction.

Lead Scoring:

Predictive analytics helps in lead scoring, a process that prioritizes leads based on their likelihood to convert into customers. By analyzing historical data and current lead interactions, AI algorithms can assign scores indicating the readiness of a lead to make a purchase. Marketing and sales teams can then focus their efforts on leads with higher scores, optimizing resource allocation and improving the efficiency of the sales pipeline.

Churn Prediction:

Churn prediction is a vital application of predictive analytics, particularly in subscription-based services and industries with recurring revenue models. Predictive models can analyze customer behavior patterns and identify signals indicating an increased risk of customer churn. By foreseeing potential churners, businesses can implement proactive retention strategies, such as targeted offers, personalized communication, or enhanced customer support, to mitigate churn and retain valuable customers.

Success Stories and Case Studies:

Numerous success stories highlight the effectiveness of predictive analytics in marketing. For instance, Netflix, a leader in the streaming industry, leverages predictive analytics to recommend content to users based on their viewing history and preferences. This has significantly contributed to their user satisfaction and retention, showcasing the power of personalized recommendations.

Similarly, Adobe, a prominent software company, utilizes predictive analytics to segment their audience and optimize their email marketing campaigns. By tailoring content and timing based on predictive models, they witnessed a substantial increase in engagement and conversion rates, underscoring the impact of predictive analytics on campaign effectiveness and ROI.

Predictive analytics in marketing has evolved beyond a mere forecasting tool. Its applications, including customer segmentation, lead scoring, and churn prediction, demonstrate its transformative potential. Real-world success stories validate its effectiveness, emphasizing its pivotal role in crafting targeted, impactful marketing strategies that yield superior results and drive business growth.

Predictive analytics, despite its transformative potential, is not without challenges and ethical considerations, particularly in the domain of marketing.

Challenges:

Data Quality and Accuracy:

One of the fundamental challenges in predictive analytics is ensuring the quality and accuracy of the data being used. Inaccurate or incomplete data can lead to flawed predictions, rendering the entire process ineffective. Data cleaning, normalization, and validation processes are vital to address this challenge and ensure the reliability of predictive models.

Overfitting and Model Complexity:

Overfitting occurs when a predictive model is excessively complex and fits the training data too closely. This can lead to poor performance when applied to new data. Striking the right balance between model complexity and simplicity is crucial to avoid overfitting and ensure the model's effectiveness in real-world scenarios.

Ethical Considerations:

Privacy Concerns:

Predictive analytics often involve analyzing personal data to make predictions. This raises privacy concerns, especially when sensitive information is used without explicit consent. Respecting individuals' privacy rights and implementing robust data anonymization and encryption techniques are essential to mitigate these concerns.

Bias in Data and Algorithms:

Biases present in historical data can perpetuate within predictive models, leading to unfair and discriminatory outcomes. Addressing bias requires careful consideration of the data sources and rigorous evaluation of the algorithms used. Implementing fairness-aware algorithms and regularly monitoring and auditing predictive models can help minimize bias and ensure equitable outcomes.

Strategies to Mitigate Challenges and Ensure Ethical Use:

Data Quality Assurance:

Implement robust data governance practices to ensure data quality, including data validation, cleaning, and regular updates. Invest in data analytics tools that can identify inconsistencies and inaccuracies, enabling data quality assurance.

Transparency and Explainability:

Foster transparency by clearly explaining how predictive analytics is used, what data is collected, and how it influences marketing strategies. Ensure that individuals are informed and can understand the implications of predictive models on their interactions with the business.

Algorithmic Fairness Testing:

Prioritize fairness testing of predictive models, particularly in sensitive domains such as finance or hiring. Regularly assess the models for bias and fairness using appropriate metrics and techniques. Address any identified biases in the algorithm to ensure fair treatment of all individuals.

Embracing predictive analytics in marketing comes with the responsibility of addressing challenges and ethical considerations. By ensuring data quality, mitigating biases, and upholding privacy, businesses can employ predictive analytics ethically, enhancing the effectiveness of marketing strategies while maintaining respect for individuals' rights and interests.

Chapter 5 : Chatbots

Chatbots, a fusion of 'chat' and 'robots,' represent a technological marvel designed to simulate human conversation. In the realm of customer interactions, they play a pivotal role as computer programs engineered to interact with users in a conversational manner. The fundamental function of chatbots is to facilitate seamless communication, acting as an intermediary between individuals and the systems or services they wish to engage with. By doing so, they emulate human-like interactions, enhancing user experience and providing a sense of personalized engagement.

When delving into the core of how chatbots operate, Artificial Intelligence (AI) and Natural Language Processing (NLP) come to the forefront. AI is the driving force behind chatbots, endowing them with the capability to learn, adapt, and respond based on data inputs and user interactions. NLP, a vital component, equips chatbots with the ability to comprehend and interpret human language, encompassing subtleties, context, and sentiment. This blend of AI and NLP empowers chatbots to engage in meaningful, contextually relevant conversations, akin to how humans communicate.

The applications of chatbots are diverse and far-reaching, revolutionizing customer interactions across various domains. In the realm of customer service, chatbots function as dependable assistants, promptly addressing common queries and concerns. They guide users through processes, provide support, and significantly improve user satisfaction. Venturing into the domain of sales, chatbots streamline the sales process by engaging potential leads, recommending products based on preferences, and facilitating transactions. In customer support, they become indispensable, efficiently handling inquiries, resolving issues, and even seamlessly escalating complex problems to human agents when necessary.

To shed light on the real-world impact, consider the integration of chatbots in e-commerce platforms. A prospective customer browsing an online store might encounter a chatbot offering personalized product recommendations based on their browsing history and preferences. This simple yet effective engagement greatly influences purchase decisions and significantly enhances the overall shopping experience. Likewise, in customer service scenarios, chatbots integrated into websites swiftly address common user queries, offering instant assistance and augmenting user navigation.

Understanding the basics of chatbots is paramount in comprehending their transformative potential within customer interactions. These AI-powered entities transcend the realm of mere computer programs; they epitomize a shift towards more conversational, efficient, and personalized engagement. In a world where interaction and assistance are becoming increasingly seamless, chatbots stand at the forefront, showcasing the fusion of technology and human-like engagement.

In the realm of chatbots, design is a linchpin, determining the success of user engagement and satisfaction. Key design principles orchestrate the user's experience, aiming for intuitiveness, seamlessness, and enjoyment. Conversational design, a foundational principle, guides the chatbot's language and flow to mimic a natural and engaging human-like conversation. User interfaces (UI) are equally vital, dictating the visual and interactive aspects of the chatbot. A well-structured UI aids in effortless navigation and interaction. Moreover, ease of use is a fundamental principle, ensuring the chatbot's simplicity and user-friendliness, crucial in preventing user overwhelm.

The impact of conversational design and UI on engagement is profound. Conversational design directly influences the user's perception and interaction, facilitating a seamless and engaging exchange of information. An intuitive conversation design significantly enhances engagement, encouraging users to stay involved and find value in the chatbot's responses. Likewise, a thoughtfully designed UI considerably influences engagement by presenting information in a clear, visually appealing manner. A clutter-free UI fosters a positive user experience, aiding smooth navigation and interaction.

To exemplify effective design, notable well-designed chatbots showcase the fusion of conversational design, intuitive UI, and ease of use. For instance, the Duolingo chatbot impeccably engages users in a conversational manner, providing effective language learning assistance. The user-friendly interface simplifies navigation, presenting a chat-like layout that resembles a friendly conversation. Another prime example is the Sephora Virtual Artist chatbot, delivering a personalized and visually appealing UI to assist users in virtually trying out makeup. These chatbots epitomize effective design, seamlessly blending conversational elements and UI to elevate customer interactions.

Adhering to design principles is pivotal in crafting a chatbot that not only users interact with but genuinely enjoy engaging with. These principles steer the creation of experiences that transcend mere interactions with a machine, resembling conversations, and ultimately enhancing the overall customer experience.

Chatbots are at the forefront of revolutionizing customer service across diverse industries, fundamentally transforming how businesses interact with their clientele. From retail to healthcare, and finance to travel, chatbots are making significant strides in providing seamless and efficient customer support. Their impact is profound, enhancing the overall customer service landscape.

Incorporating chatbots in customer service processes yields an array of benefits. Chatbots operate 24/7, ensuring round-the-clock availability to assist customers, a feat often unattainable with human support. They handle a myriad of common customer inquiries, complaints, and support requests promptly and accurately. This not only alleviates the workload on human agents but also ensures quick responses, augmenting customer satisfaction. Furthermore, chatbots maintain a consistent tone and quality of responses, enhancing the brand image by delivering standardized and professional interactions.

To exemplify the transformation, consider a case study in the e-commerce industry. An online retail giant integrated a chatbot into its customer service system, addressing customer inquiries about products, order status, and returns. The chatbot efficiently handled a significant volume of inquiries, providing instant responses and guiding customers through processes. This not only reduced the burden on human agents but also led to a remarkable improvement in customer satisfaction, with customers appreciating the speed and accuracy of the chatbot's assistance.

In another case within the healthcare sector, a leading telemedicine platform deployed a chatbot to provide initial assistance to patients seeking medical advice. The chatbot effectively triaged symptoms, offering recommendations on further actions and scheduling appointments with appropriate healthcare professionals. This implementation significantly expedited the initial consultation process, ensuring timely medical attention for patients and enhancing their overall healthcare experience.

These case studies serve as testaments to the tangible improvements in customer service through chatbot integration. They underscore the potential of chatbots in streamlining customer interactions, boosting efficiency, and ultimately elevating customer satisfaction across diverse industries.

In the dynamic landscape of sales and e-commerce, chatbots have emerged as game-changers, profoundly influencing the sales processes and elevating the overall shopping experience for customers. Their integration has disrupted traditional sales methods, adding efficiency, personalization, and speed to the sales journey.

Chatbots play a pivotal role in transforming sales processes by automating and expediting various stages. From the initial engagement with potential customers to guiding them through product options and ultimately facilitating the purchase, chatbots streamline the entire process. They act as proactive assistants, readily available to address inquiries, provide product information, and assist with the decision-making process.

One of the key contributions of chatbots is their role in lead generation. Through strategic interactions, they gather essential information from prospective customers, qualify leads, and route them to the appropriate sales channels. This not only optimizes the lead generation process but also ensures that sales teams focus on qualified and potentially high-converting leads.

Additionally, chatbots excel in offering personalized product recommendations based on customer preferences, browsing history, and purchase patterns. By understanding the customer's needs and preferences, chatbots guide them to suitable products, enhancing their shopping experience. This personalization significantly influences purchase decisions, leading to increased sales and customer satisfaction.

Real-life examples further emphasize the transformative impact of chatbots in e-commerce. Consider a renowned online fashion retailer that integrated a chatbot into its platform. The chatbot engaged customers in conversations about their style preferences, occasions, and clothing requirements. Based on this input, it provided tailored product recommendations, resulting in a notable surge in sales and improved customer engagement.

In another instance, a leading electronics e-commerce platform deployed a chatbot to assist customers in understanding complex technical specifications of products. The chatbot simplified the information, ensuring customers made informed decisions. This not only reduced the burden on customer service but also led to a rise in successful order processing and customer satisfaction.

These examples underscore how chatbots are revolutionizing sales in e-commerce, showcasing their potential to significantly impact sales figures, enhance customer engagement, and redefine the shopping experience.

Chapter 6 : AI in Content Creatio

AI-generated content represents a significant milestone in the intersection of technology and creativity. The mechanisms behind AI-generated content heavily rely on two key components: natural language processing (NLP) and machine learning (ML) algorithms. Natural language processing enables AI to understand, interpret, and generate human language in a manner that is coherent and contextually relevant. It involves syntactic and semantic analysis, enabling AI to comprehend the intricacies of grammar, style, and meaning. Machine learning algorithms, on the other hand, learn from vast amounts of data to mimic human-like language patterns and structures, allowing AI to generate content that appears human-created.

The current capabilities of AI in generating diverse types of content are substantial. AI can now create articles, blog posts, social media updates, and even poetry with a level of coherence and quality that often surprises. However, it's essential to acknowledge the limitations. AI-generated content often lacks true understanding and consciousness, resulting in occasional inaccuracies, incoherence, or misrepresentations. It may lack the deeper insights and emotions that human-generated content naturally possesses.

Despite these limitations, AI-generated content holds immense potential, especially in the realm of content marketing. It can automate the generation of content for marketing campaigns, tailoring it to specific target audiences. AI can swiftly produce a volume of content, aiding in brand visibility and engagement. For instance, AI can create personalized email marketing campaigns, generate product descriptions for e-commerce websites, or even draft engaging social media posts. This potential to scale and customize content creation is where AI showcases its relevance in content marketing strategies.

AI-generated content is a burgeoning field empowered by natural language processing and machine learning. It can mimic human language patterns and create a diverse array of content. However, striking a balance between efficiency and human touch is vital, recognizing the capabilities and limitations of AI-generated content.

Effective curation of AI-generated content is a vital step to ensure its quality, relevance, and alignment with brand identity. While AI can produce content at scale, human intervention is crucial to refine and elevate the quality of the generated material. Strategies for curation involve establishing clear guidelines and parameters for the AI algorithms, guiding them to create content that aligns with the brand's tone, style, and messaging. Regular review and feedback loops are essential to iteratively improve the AI's output, ensuring it meets the desired standards.

The importance of human intervention in the curation process cannot be overstated. Human oversight is instrumental in fine-tuning the AI-generated content to resonate with the target audience. Human curators possess the creative insight and understanding of the brand's ethos, enabling them to add a personal touch, emotional depth, and nuance to the AI-generated material. They can imbue the content with authenticity, ensuring it appeals to the audience in a genuine and relatable manner.

To illustrate the effectiveness of curated AI-generated content, let's consider a case study in the realm of social media marketing. A leading technology company integrated AI to generate content for their social media posts. While the AI effectively produced content, human curators were pivotal in the curation process. They fine-tuned the AI-generated material, aligning it with the brand's voice and values. This curated content demonstrated a noticeable improvement in audience engagement, indicating the effectiveness of human-guided curation in enhancing AI-generated content's impact.

In another instance, an e-commerce platform utilized AI to generate product descriptions. Human curators meticulously refined and personalized the AI-generated descriptions, ensuring they captured the essence and unique selling points of each product. This curated AI-generated content significantly influenced purchase decisions, leading to a notable increase in sales and customer satisfaction.

These case studies underscore the symbiotic relationship between AI-generated content and human curation. Effective curation not only enhances the quality of AI-generated material but also maximizes its impact on audience engagement and ultimately, business outcomes.

As AI-generated content becomes increasingly prevalent, navigating the ethical landscape is paramount. The rise of AI brings to light ethical implications concerning authenticity, bias, transparency, and responsible utilization. Authenticity is a crucial concern, as AI-generated content can sometimes mislead readers into believing it's human-generated. Striking a balance between

AI's capabilities and maintaining authenticity is a delicate yet essential ethical consideration.

Bias in AI-generated content is another critical issue. AI algorithms learn from historical data, potentially perpetuating biases present in that data. Biased content can reinforce stereotypes or present skewed perspectives. Recognizing and mitigating biases is vital to ensure that AI-generated content remains fair and inclusive, reflecting the diversity of perspectives and voices.

Ensuring transparency in AI-generated content is an ethical imperative. Users have the right to know if they are interacting with content created by AI. Clear labeling helps in maintaining transparency, fostering trust and enabling users to make informed judgments regarding the content they consume.

The responsibility of organizations and content creators is central in guiding the ethical use of AI-generated content. It's imperative to emphasize the importance of using AI to augment human creativity rather than replace it entirely. Content creators should wield AI as a tool, infusing it with human values, oversight, and creativity to ensure the content aligns with ethical standards and societal norms.

To uphold ethical principles, organizations should propose ethical guidelines for utilizing AI in content creation and curation. These guidelines should emphasize authenticity, encourage bias detection and mitigation, promote transparency, and advocate for responsible AI usage. They should be dynamic, adapting to advancements in AI technology and emerging ethical challenges.

Navigating the ethical considerations in AI-generated content is a complex task that demands vigilance and responsibility. Ethical awareness and adherence are essential in leveraging AI's potential to enhance content creation while preserving trust, credibility, and societal values.

The future of AI in content creation is poised to be revolutionary, shaping the landscape of creative expression. Advancements in AI are expected to significantly impact how content is generated, curated, and consumed. AI's ability to comprehend and replicate human language and creativity is projected to improve, resulting in more sophisticated and convincing AI-generated content.

One of the most exciting prospects is the potential for creative collaboration between AI and humans. AI can assist human creators by suggesting ideas, providing frameworks, and automating repetitive tasks. This collaboration can amplify creativity and productivity, allowing humans to focus on higher-level creative aspects while AI handles the groundwork. Moreover, AI's ability to comprehend and interpret vast amounts of data can inspire innovative approaches and novel perspectives for human creators.

The integration of AI in content creation is likely to bring about disruptions and innovations in the traditional content creation industry. AI's efficiency in generating content at scale and its capacity to personalize content for specific target audiences will alter conventional workflows and strategies. Content creators and industries will need to adapt to this shift, embracing AI as a tool for enhancing creativity and meeting the evolving demands of the audience.

AI-generated content will not be confined to conventional platforms. The emergence of virtual reality (VR), augmented reality (AR), and mixed reality (MR) will open new avenues for AI-generated immersive content. AI can play a pivotal role in creating interactive and engaging experiences within these technologies, enhancing storytelling and user engagement. This represents a significant frontier where AI-generated content will intersect with cutting-edge technologies, reshaping the future of storytelling and user experiences.

The future of AI in content creation holds immense potential for reshaping how content is created, curated, and experienced. Advancements, collaborative possibilities, disruptions in traditional workflows, and integration with emerging technologies all contribute to a promising landscape where AI augments human creativity and propels the content creation domain into uncharted territories.

Chapter 7 : Ethical Considerations

The integration of AI in marketing raises significant privacy concerns, primarily regarding the handling and processing of customer data. AI technologies heavily rely on data, and in the marketing context, this often means collecting and analyzing vast amounts of personal information. This collection can be perceived as intrusive, as it may involve tracking online behavior, preferences, and sometimes even sensitive data.

The handling of customer data by AI technologies can potentially infringe on privacy. Customers might be unaware of the extent to which their information is being used and might not have given explicit consent for certain types of data processing. There's a delicate balance between utilizing customer data to enhance marketing strategies and respecting individuals' privacy rights.

To address these privacy concerns, it is crucial to propose effective strategies and technologies. Firstly, transparency in data usage is key. Companies must clearly communicate to customers how their data will be used and seek consent for each specific purpose. Implementing privacy-by-design principles ensures that privacy is considered at every stage of AI application development. Moreover, utilizing privacy-enhancing technologies like data anonymization and encryption can help protect individuals' privacy while still allowing for effective data analysis and utilization in AI-driven marketing campaigns.

Navigating privacy concerns in AI marketing necessitates a thoughtful and ethical approach. Respecting individuals' privacy while leveraging the power of AI to enhance marketing effectiveness is a delicate yet crucial balance that businesses must achieve.

Responsible use of customer data lies at the heart of ethical AI marketing strategies. When incorporating AI into marketing strategies, it's imperative to consider the ethical dimensions related to the collection, storage, and utilization of customer data. This involves a thorough understanding and implementation of guidelines and best practices.

A fundamental aspect of responsible data use is ensuring that data collection, storage, and utilization prioritize customer consent and data security. Companies should transparently inform customers about the types of data collected and the purpose behind it. Consent should be obtained for each specific use of the data, and customers should have the option to opt out or modify their consent preferences.

Data security is another critical concern. Implementing robust security measures to safeguard customer data from unauthorized access or breaches is non-negotiable. This includes encryption, access controls, and regular security audits.

To further promote responsible use of customer data, mechanisms should be in place to educate consumers about how their data is used. This can be achieved through clear and concise privacy policies, educational campaigns, and accessible resources. Empowering consumers with knowledge about their data's use allows them to make informed decisions and reinforces trust in the organization.

Moreover, providing consumers with control over their information is vital. Giving them the ability to access, edit, or delete their data ensures they maintain ownership and agency over their information. Such control mechanisms could be facilitated through user-friendly interfaces and transparent data management practices.

Responsible use of customer data involves meticulous attention to ethical guidelines, obtaining consent, ensuring data security, educating consumers, and granting them control over their information. These practices are essential in building and maintaining trust between businesses and their customers in the AI-driven marketing landscape.

Adhering to ethical standards and regulatory requirements is paramount in the realm of AI marketing. It's a testament to an organization's commitment to responsible practices and respect for both customers and the law. Ethical compliance not only safeguards consumers but also fosters a sense of trust and credibility.

Highlighting the importance of complying with ethical standards and regulations in AI marketing, businesses must recognize that compliance is not a choice but a necessity. Regulatory bodies and authorities set forth guidelines to ensure fairness, transparency, and ethical conduct in AI applications. Non-compliance not only carries legal repercussions but can also lead to reputational damage and loss of consumer trust.

Discussing key regulatory frameworks and guidelines concerning AI-driven marketing practices is essential to educate businesses. Understanding laws such as the General Data Protection Regulation (GDPR) in Europe or the California Consumer Privacy Act (CCPA) in the United States is critical. These frameworks emphasize data protection, privacy, and consent, aligning with ethical considerations.

Exploring how businesses can ensure adherence to these regulations while maximizing the benefits of AI is a balancing act. Educating teams on compliance, integrating compliance into the AI development life cycle, and conducting regular audits are steps towards ensuring adherence. Additionally, employing AI systems that are designed with privacy by design can naturally align with these regulations.

Businesses need to adopt a proactive approach, staying informed about evolving regulations, adapting their AI marketing strategies accordingly, and integrating ethical compliance into their core values and practices. In doing so, they not only demonstrate responsibility but also create a competitive advantage by earning consumer trust and goodwill.

Ethical compliance and regulatory adherence are foundational in AI marketing. They establish a framework of trust and responsibility, benefiting both businesses and consumers. Understanding, embracing, and proactively implementing these standards is vital for a sustainable and ethical AI-driven marketing landscape.

Addressing biases present in AI algorithms is paramount for ensuring fairness and inclusivity in AI marketing. Bias can manifest within AI algorithms due to skewed training data or inherent biases within the algorithms themselves. These biases can lead to unequal treatment and discriminatory outcomes.

Delving into the potential biases present in AI marketing algorithms, it's crucial to recognize that biases can arise from historical data that reflects societal prejudices. This perpetuates existing biases in marketing efforts, potentially reinforcing stereotypes or excluding certain demographic groups. The ethical implications are profound, as biased marketing algorithms can contribute to an unfair advantage for specific segments of the population while disadvantaging others.

Discussing strategies to detect, mitigate, and eliminate biases is essential. Bias detection mechanisms should be integrated into AI marketing algorithms, involving thorough testing and evaluation. Mitigation strategies may include re-evaluating training data, adjusting algorithms, or employing post-processing techniques to correct biases.

Moreover, it's crucial to emphasize the role of diversity and inclusion in AI development to create unbiased marketing technologies. Diverse teams, representative of various backgrounds and perspectives, can contribute to reducing biases. By incorporating diverse viewpoints and experiences during AI algorithm design and development, it's possible to identify and rectify biases effectively.

Addressing biases and promoting fairness in AI marketing algorithms is a critical ethical concern. By acknowledging the potential biases, implementing effective detection and mitigation strategies, and promoting diversity and inclusion, we can strive to ensure that AI-driven marketing is fair, inclusive, and reflective of the diverse audience it serves.

Chapter 8 : The Road Ahead

The fusion of AI with augmented reality (AR) represents an incredibly promising frontier in marketing strategies. Integrating AI and AR opens a gateway to unparalleled customer experiences and engagement across diverse marketing contexts. AI's analytical prowess combined with AR's immersive and interactive nature can create a dynamic marketing landscape.

This integration holds immense potential to enhance customer experiences. By leveraging AI capabilities within AR, marketers can personalize and tailor experiences to individual preferences. Imagine a scenario where AR glasses powered by AI recognize a consumer in a store and provide real-time, personalized product recommendations based on their previous purchases and preferences. This level of personalization can significantly influence purchasing decisions and overall satisfaction.

Moreover, the fusion of AI and AR can lead to unprecedented engagement. Interactive advertisements and campaigns powered by AI-driven AR can captivate audiences and encourage active participation. For instance, consumers can virtually try on products, visualize how furniture would fit in their homes, or even take part in gamified marketing experiences, all facilitated by AI algorithms enhancing the AR interface.

To provide a tangible sense of this potential, let's look at a successful implementation. A prominent example is IKEA's AR app, where customers can use their smartphones to visualize how different pieces of furniture would look in their homes. AI algorithms help in suggesting complementary items and understanding user preferences, offering a seamless and personalized shopping experience.

The fusion of AI with AR represents a paradigm shift in marketing. It has the power to redefine how customers interact with products and services, providing an immersive and tailored experience. The examples of successful implementations illustrate the transformative impact this fusion can have on the future of marketing strategies.

The emergence and integration of AI-powered voice search technologies are revolutionizing marketing strategies in profound ways. AI has become pivotal in processing and responding to voice commands, enabling devices like smartphones, smart speakers, and other IoT devices to understand and execute spoken requests. This evolution is significantly altering how consumers interact with brands and make purchase decisions.

AI's role in voice search is reshaping consumer interactions and purchase behaviors. Voice search offers a more natural and convenient way for consumers to seek information or perform tasks.

Whether it's searching for a product, asking for directions, or even making a purchase, the ease of using voice commands fosters a seamless and efficient user experience. Consumers are increasingly turning to voice search for quick answers and recommendations.

This shift has substantial implications for marketing strategies. SEO and content optimization are adapting to accommodate voice search. Conversational and long-tail keywords, natural language processing, and featured snippets are becoming critical in optimizing content for voice-based queries. Marketers are now focusing on creating content that aligns with how people speak, ensuring their brands are visible and accessible in voice search results.

Looking into the future, AI-powered voice search is expected to continue evolving. Improved accuracy and context-aware responses will enhance the user experience, making voice search even more integral to daily life. In marketing, this means brands must optimize not just for keywords but for understanding the nuances of human speech and intent.

AI's integration into voice search technologies is transforming marketing strategies. As the technology advances, understanding and adapting to this shift becomes essential. Marketers need to embrace the nuances of voice search, optimizing content and strategies to align with the future where voice interactions play a central role in consumer engagement.

Recent years have witnessed a rapid evolution of AI-driven advertising, heralding a paradigm shift in how brands engage with their target audiences. Programmatic advertising, one of the notable advancements, leverages AI algorithms to automate the buying of ads and target them more precisely. This ensures that each impression is maximized for relevance and effectiveness, optimizing ad spend.

Dynamic content optimization is another groundbreaking advancement. AI empowers marketers to tailor content dynamically based on user behavior and preferences. Personalized advertising at scale has become feasible, allowing brands to deliver individualized messages to a diverse audience. AI algorithms analyze data and generate content variations, ensuring that the right message reaches the right person at the right time.

Furthermore, AI's role in ad targeting precision has become indispensable. AI algorithms analyze massive datasets to identify patterns, behaviors, and preferences. This enables advertisers to precisely target their ads to individuals or segments most likely to respond positively, enhancing engagement and conversion rates.

Looking forward, the future of AI-driven advertising holds exciting prospects. Predictive analytics and AI-powered customer insights are anticipated to play a more significant role, allowing advertisers to foresee consumer behavior and tailor campaigns accordingly. Additionally, AI may facilitate interactive and immersive advertisements, enabling customers to engage with products virtually before making a purchase decision.

AI-driven advertising has made substantial strides, with programmatic advertising, dynamic content optimization, and precise ad targeting being at the forefront. The future promises even more transformative advancements, empowering advertisers to anticipate consumer behavior and create engaging, immersive experiences.

In the age of big data, AI stands as the linchpin, ready to harness and make sense of the immense volume of data generated daily. The deluge of data, from social media interactions to online transactions, necessitates sophisticated tools and techniques for analysis and interpretation. This is where AI steps in, poised to transform how we handle and derive insights from this vast reservoir of information.

The potential of AI in optimizing data analysis for targeted marketing campaigns is immense. AI-powered analytics tools, equipped with machine learning algorithms, can swiftly process and analyze large datasets to identify patterns, trends, and consumer behaviors. This enables marketers to make data-driven decisions, optimizing campaigns to resonate with their target audience.

Consumer personalization, a cornerstone of modern marketing, is greatly amplified by AI. AI algorithms can segment audiences based on diverse parameters, allowing for hyper-personalized marketing strategies. The understanding derived from big data, facilitated by AI, ensures that every marketing communication is highly relevant and engaging, fostering stronger customer relationships.

As we look ahead, AI's role in managing big data is only expected to grow. Predictive analytics, leveraging AI, will provide businesses with invaluable foresights into consumer preferences and future market trends. AI-driven data management will become more sophisticated, ensuring data privacy, security, and compliance with regulatory standards.

The impact of AI on the marketing landscape, in the age of big data, is profound. It's no longer about the quantity of data but the quality of insights derived from it. AI is a powerful catalyst, propelling marketing strategies towards being more precise, personalized, and efficient.

AI's potential in managing big data and deriving actionable insights will be a hallmark of successful marketing strategies in the future. It's a symbiotic relationship; as data grows, so does AI's capability to make that data work for us.

The rapid advancements in AI present a double-edged sword in the realm of marketing, invoking a host of ethical considerations. As AI technologies penetrate deeper into our lives and influence our decisions, the responsible and ethical use of these technologies becomes imperative.

One of the significant ethical considerations revolves around consumer privacy. The abundance of consumer data being collected raises concerns about how this data is handled and whether it's used in a manner that respects individual privacy. AI algorithms often rely on extensive data, and ensuring this data is anonymized and securely stored is vital.

Additionally, there's a notable concern about bias and fairness in AI algorithms. AI models learn from historical data, and if this data is biased, the AI may perpetuate and even exacerbate existing biases. Ensuring fairness and inclusivity in the outcomes of AI algorithms is a critical ethical challenge.

Misuse of AI in advertising and consumer targeting poses another ethical risk. Hyper-targeted advertisements have the potential to exploit vulnerabilities or manipulate consumer behaviors. Striking a balance between effective targeting and ethical boundaries is vital to ensure that AI-driven advertising remains transparent and respects consumer rights.

To mitigate these ethical concerns, strategies need to be in place. Transparency should be at the core, with businesses being transparent about how they use AI and data. Ethics training and guidelines for AI practitioners can instill an ethical mindset, promoting responsible AI development and deployment. Regulatory frameworks that set the boundaries for AI use in marketing can also provide a strong foundation for ethical practices.

The ethical implications of AI advancements in marketing are profound. Striking the right balance between leveraging AI's capabilities and ensuring ethical use is crucial to building trust with consumers and ensuring a sustainable and responsible future for AI in marketing.

Chapter 9 : Implementing AI in Marketing

Integrating AI into a marketing strategy is a significant step that requires a solid foundation. Key indicators can help organizations gauge their readiness for this integration. Firstly, a willingness to invest in AI and allocate adequate resources is crucial. Organizations ready for AI understand the value it adds and are committed to supporting it effectively.

Technological infrastructure and data capabilities are foundational. Evaluating the existing infrastructure to determine if it can seamlessly integrate with AI systems is vital. The ability to collect, store, and process data efficiently is a strong indicator of readiness. Data quality and accessibility are equally important; having clean, structured data that can be readily utilized in AI processes is a good sign.

Successful AI integrations often have common factors contributing to their success. Organizations that thrive in AI integration often have a culture of adaptability and continuous learning. They encourage employees to upskill and stay updated with AI advancements. Additionally, having clear communication channels and collaboration among departments, especially between marketing and IT, can greatly contribute to the success of AI integration.

Assessing organizational readiness for AI integration involves evaluating the willingness to invest, the adequacy of technological infrastructure and data capabilities, and fostering a culture of adaptability and collaboration. Successful AI integrations are often underpinned by a holistic approach that involves both technological readiness and an organizational mindset conducive to AI adoption.

Integrating AI into a marketing strategy requires a well-thought-out approach. Step-by-step strategies are fundamental to ensure a smooth and effective integration. Firstly, it's essential to conduct a comprehensive audit of existing marketing processes and identify areas where AI can make a significant impact. Understanding specific pain points helps tailor AI solutions accordingly.

Aligning AI initiatives with the overall business goals is pivotal. Exploring this alignment involves ensuring that AI applications directly contribute to achieving broader organizational objectives. For instance, if the goal is to enhance customer engagement, AI can be employed to create personalized customer experiences through targeted marketing campaigns.

Change management strategies play a crucial role in the success of AI integration. Insights into effective change management include involving employees early in the process, providing adequate training and resources, and fostering a culture that embraces change. It's about preparing the organization for a shift, ensuring everyone understands the value AI brings, and is equipped to work effectively with AI-driven processes.

Successful implementation of AI in marketing entails step-by-step strategies that involve auditing existing processes, aligning AI initiatives with broader business goals, and employing effective change management strategies. A systematic approach, combined with alignment and change readiness, sets the stage for a successful integration of AI into marketing strategies.

Measuring the impact of AI on marketing ROI is crucial for understanding the effectiveness of AI integration. Delving into methodologies and key metrics provides a comprehensive view of this impact. Metrics can vary based on organizational goals, but common indicators include customer engagement metrics, lead generation rates, conversion rates, and ultimately, the return on investment.

AI has a substantial influence on customer engagement. By providing personalized and relevant content to individual customers, AI enhances engagement rates. Measuring this engagement shift, whether through increased interactions, time spent on a website, or social media interactions, can be indicative of AI's impact.

Lead generation is a fundamental aspect of marketing. AI can optimize lead generation by identifying and targeting potential leads more effectively. Metrics such as the increase in lead quality, lead conversion rates, and the time taken to convert leads can showcase AI's contribution to this vital marketing KPI.

Conversion rates are a direct reflection of marketing effectiveness. AI's influence on conversion rates can be measured through A/B testing, analyzing customer journeys, and tracking conversion paths. Comparing pre-AI and post-AI implementation conversion rates provides insights into the effectiveness of AI in conversion optimization.

Real-world examples and case studies further highlight the impact of AI on marketing ROI. These studies could showcase scenarios where AI-led personalization significantly increased engagement, improved lead quality, or boosted conversion rates, ultimately contributing to a measurable improvement in marketing ROI.

Measuring AI's impact on marketing ROI involves utilizing appropriate methodologies and key metrics related to customer engagement, lead generation, conversion rates, and more. Case studies provide tangible evidence of AI's potential to drive significant improvements in marketing ROI.

Integrating AI into a marketing strategy comes with its set of challenges. Identifying common challenges is crucial for effective integration. Some of these challenges include the high cost of implementation, resistance to change within the organization, difficulty in finding the right AI talent, and concerns about data privacy and security.

Discussing potential solutions and best practices to overcome these challenges is essential. For instance, addressing the cost challenge can involve starting with smaller AI projects and gradually scaling up. To combat resistance to change, organizations can invest in comprehensive training programs to upskill employees and create a culture that embraces technological advancements.

Real-world examples of organizations that have successfully navigated these challenges are invaluable. Sharing such examples can inspire and provide insights into effective strategies. For instance, a company struggling with finding the right AI talent might collaborate with AI-focused educational institutions or partner with AI consulting firms to bridge the talent gap effectively.

Addressing challenges in AI integration involves identifying common hurdles, discussing potential solutions and best practices, and sharing real-world examples of successful navigation through these challenges. A proactive approach and learning from others' experiences are fundamental in overcoming obstacles and ensuring a smooth integration of AI into marketing strategies.

Integrating AI into your marketing strategy can be a game-changer. Summarizing actionable insights and recommendations for this integration is key. Firstly, start with a clear understanding of your marketing objectives and how AI can support them. Align AI initiatives with specific goals to derive the maximum benefit.

Selecting the right AI tools and platforms is critical. Providing tips for this selection involves considering factors like the tool's relevance to your industry, ease of integration, scalability, and vendor support. Evaluating these aspects ensures a compatible fit and effective utilization of AI capabilities.

Collaboration is key for successful integration. Sharing best practices for maintaining a culture of continuous improvement emphasizes fostering an environment that encourages innovation and experimentation. Encourage cross-functional teams to work closely, exchange insights, and share learnings from AI integration experiences, ensuring ongoing growth and adaptation.

Successful AI integration in marketing demands a clear alignment of AI initiatives with marketing goals, careful selection of AI tools and partners, and fostering a culture of continuous improvement and innovation. By embracing these principles, businesses can maximize the benefits of AI and drive growth in their marketing strategies.

hebooks